THE ART OF
WRITING

陸機

文賦

THE ART OF
WRITING

Lu Chi's
Wen Fu

TRANSLATED FROM THE CHINESE BY
SAM HAMILL

MILKWEED EDITIONS

Published 2000 by Milkweed Editions
Printed in Canada by Friesens Corporation
Cover design by redletterdesign.com
Cover photograph by Darren Rob, courtesy of Tony Stone
Interior design by Elizabeth Cleveland
Chinese calligraphy, "Lu Chi Wen Fu," by Stephen Addiss
The text of this book is set in Cochin.
15   16   17   18   8   7   6   5
Revised Edition 2000

Milkweed Editions, a nonprofit publisher, gratefully acknowledges support
from the Elmer L. and Eleanor J. Andersen Foundation; James Ford Bell
Foundation; Bush Foundation; General Mills Foundation; Honeywell
Foundation; Jerome Foundation; McKnight Foundation; Minnesota State
Arts Board through an appropriation by the Minnesota State Legislature;
Norwest Foundation on behalf of Norwest Bank Minnesota; Lawrence
and Elizabeth Ann O'Shaughnessy Charitable Income Trust in honor of
Lawrence M. O'Shaughnessy; Oswald Family Foundation; Ritz Foundation
on behalf of Mr. and Mrs. E. J. Phelps Jr.; John and Beverly Rollwagen
Fund of the Minneapolis Foundation; St. Paul Companies, Inc.; Star
Tribune Foundation; Target Foundation on behalf of Dayton's, Mervyn's
California and Target Stores; U.S. Bancorp Piper Jaffray Foundation on
behalf of U.S. Bancorp Piper Jaffray; and generous individuals.

Library of Congress Cataloging-in-Publication Data

Lu Chi, 261–303.
   [Wen fu. English]
   The art of writing : Lu Chi's Wen Fu / translated by Sam Hamill.
      p.   cm.
   Translation of: Wen fu.
   ISBN 1-57131-412-1
   1. Chinese literature — History and criticism — Theory, etc.
   I. Hamill, Sam.
   PL2261.L8413 1991
   808'.04951 — dc20   90-25970
                                                                      CIP

This book is printed on acid-free paper.

To Eron Hamill and Gray Foster
And to Hayden Carruth

THE ART OF
WRITING

How much I desire!
Inside my little satchel,
the moon, and flowers

— Bashō

PREFACE TO THE 2000 EDITION

The earliest version of this translation was published by *The American Poetry Review* in 1987. First book publication, limited to two hundred signed copies, was produced by Barbarian Press of British Columbia, also in 1987, and was followed by a trade edition published by Breitenbush Books, in early 1988. The first revised edition was issued by Milkweed Editions in 1991, and with that, *The Art of Writing* has, happily, remained in print for nearly ten years. I am grateful to Emilie Buchwald and Milkweed Editions for welcoming this new revision, and for bringing Lu Chi's classic back into the English-speaking world in a new edition to coincide with publication of my *Crossing the Yellow River: Three Hundred Poems from the Chinese* (BOA

Editions). Lu Chi's essay is not only essential to the understanding of Chinese poetry, but to the whole writing process.

In our own time, it is all but impossible to imagine actually putting one's life in jeopardy over a poem or essay, but to the classical Chinese poet, it was a daily reality unless one was willing to play cozy with the ruling class. But even then, a revolution could spring up at almost any moment, and last year's prizewinner could very well be this year's ritual sacrifice or exile. There are few major classical Chinese poets who did not experience exile at one time or another.

Such conditions have been an essential element in the history of poetry in the West as well. Socrates provides our archetype. Dante wrote his comedy under a death sentence. As I write, I think of Czeslaw Milosz and Ha Jin and dozens of other poets from around the world who have sought refugee status in the United States. Lu Chi wrote his treatise for them, and for all those who dare to engage poetry, the art of letters, at its deepest levels. In his seriousness, there is great joy; in his instruction, there is not only a noble investigation of writing practice, but a lesson in living well.

TRANSLATOR'S INTRODUCTION

Lu Chi's *Wen Fu* is the first major discourse on the art of writing in ancient Chinese and is composed in what might best be described as "prose poetry," except that it bears little or no resemblance to what passes as prose poetry in our own language. It is written in irregular poetic lines arranged as verse paragraphs rather like those used by Allen Ginsberg in *Howl,* but rhymed. While Lu Chi was not the inventor of the *fu* form, he put it to a striking new use. Before his time the *fu* was a popular form used almost exclusively for discursive poems on historical events or for singing the praises of one's military or political rulers.

Prior to the composition of the *Wen Fu,* the first great work to discuss the use of language is the *Ta Hsueh* (or *Great Learning*) of K'ung-fu Tzu (Confucius). Master K'ung believed all wisdom lies in learning to call things by the right name, and that only through a "rectification of names" might one proceed toward enlightened living. This insight is doubly remarkable when we remember that K'ung-fu Tzu lived in a nation that was far more sophisticated than any other on earth at that time, its language rich in emblematic phrases, euphemisms, double entendres, and layered ambiguities loaded with plurisignation. The *Ta Hsueh* is one of the "Stone Classics" carved around 175 C.E., late in the Han dynasty, in the capital city of Loyang. Initially, it was part of the *Li Chi (Book of Rites)*, but became a "book" in its own right nearly seven hundred years after Lu Chi would have studied it as part of his Confucian training during the late third century.

Lao Tzu and Chuang Tzu were both fond of pointing out the fallacy of believing, as Edward Said recently asserted, that "language is where being dwells." Lao Tzu opens his *Tao Te Ching* by observing that "the way that can be named is not the Tao." Chuang Tzu pokes fun at those who call for Confucian "virtuousness." Every literate

Chinese poet was rigorously schooled in Confucian and Taoist classics. Every good poet struggled to achieve Confucian exactitude in language while understanding that Lao Tzu wrote thousands of characters explaining why language is insufficient in articulating the essential Tao.

Lu Chi was born on the Yangtze Delta in 261, shortly after the end of Hellenistic Greece. It is impossible to know whether Lu Chi knew or had heard about classical Greece, but he must have heard reports from the frontiers about the Roman Empire. As an educated man, he was probably aware of the growth of Judeo-Christian civilization throughout his westernmost neighboring communities of "barbarians." He was a scholar of the *Analects (Lun Yu)* or dialogues of Master K'ung, and of its precepts, many of which are echoed in the *Wen Fu.* "How to play music may be known. At the commencement of the piece, all the parts should sound together. As it proceeds, they should be in harmony, while severally distinct and flowing without break, and thus on to conclusion." Or, "There are some who know all the notes, and there are some who know the music." Lu Chi's essay owes a great deal, not only to the content of the *Analects,* but to its very style, and to several of its more famous metaphors and similes.

Lu Chi was the grandson of Lu Sun, himself instrumental in attaining the southern throne for the first Wu emperor and who had been rewarded with the title of Duke. Lu Chi's father was Lu K'ang, a military leader charged with responsibilities of protecting the empire from invaders from the north. The Lu family was itself from the north country, a family that had distinguished itself by producing military genius, men notable for their intense patriotism and reliability. Even so, Lu Sun's first passion was "to be a servant to the gods of the soil." Like his grandfather, Lu Chi held a deep abiding respect for the culture and landscape of the Yangtze Delta. He knew its seasons and its soils and its people.

Lu K'ang had become a military leader at nineteen and had died when Lu Chi was only twelve or thirteen, leaving six sons, at least three of whom, including Lu Chi, followed his example and entered the military. The Lu family estate was large and prosperous. They owned rice fields and mulberry groves along the delta, and bamboo groves in rolling hills near West Lake in Hangchow. A strikingly large boy, Lu grew to well over six feet.

He was extraordinarily bright, and obsessed with learning.

After his father died, he was named captain of the family troops and studied military strategy intensely for the ensuing five years. Despite Lu K'ang's many warnings about the threat of a major invasion from the north, the weak-willed Emperor Hao had neglected to reinforce the dwindling army, and when the invasion finally came, the Wu empire was decimated. The Lu brothers had predicted just such a catastrophe.

Two of Lu Chi's brothers were killed in battle, but both he and his beloved younger brother escaped and fled to Hua T'ing, where they "barred the door and devoted themselves to study." It is typical of Lu, and of Chinese genius in general, that in the face of utter defeat, he searches for solutions first within himself. The Lu brothers' self-imposed exile lasted ten long years, a decade in which they steeped themselves in the Confucian classics, in Taoist and Buddhist wisdom books, and in a thorough and detailed history of literature.

During their exile, Lu Chi wrote *Dialectic of Destruction,* describing the causes of the collapse of the Wu empire, an essay especially notable for its caustic tone and bitter assessment of the general incompetence and self-indulgence of the ruling class. Searching for the causes of calamity within himself, he finds he must finally call things by the right name, even when that means placing responsibility with the emperor or with the poet's elders. It was writing that could have gotten him killed. In a poem, "Song of Mount T'ai," he wrote:

> These foothills have known the ritual sacrifice
> of the emperor who built a pavilion.
>
> This dark trail harbors many a ghost,
> a hundred ancient spirits.

At the end of his poem, Lu Chi claims an obligation to continue to "bravely sing." This, too, could have been grounds for his execution. Nothing, it seems, could shake the poet's commitment to truth-telling as the foundation of his art. He dares question the morality of "ritual sacrifice" that had been a part of Chinese nobility for a thousand years, thereby impugning the authority of the emperor. The ghosts and spirits he calls up are those of ancient poets and seers who sought enlightenment on Mount T'ai, the center of Chinese Buddhism. Li Po and dozens of other poets of the T'ang and

Sung dynasties would write poems about the mountain, T'ai Shan, most of which echo Lu Chi in one way or another.

Finally, the two brothers returned north at the court's direction in 290 as a new court began to decentralize the government. In Lo-yang, Lu Chi was named to office as a literary secretary. But life at court proved to be a constant struggle, as it did to so very many Chinese poets. He referred to the capital as a foreign country, but managed to persevere until, in 296, he was appointed to head an army detachment to wage war against the barbarians. A deft, inspiring leader, he served well and before long became a personal secretary to the emperor. But the Fates were not kind: the emperor lacked both discipline and imagination, and the country was quickly torn apart by the competitive plotting of the eight princes.

In the year 300, the Prince of Chao began a six-year open war by destroying the entire palace administration. Lu Chi's troops were confronted by an army led by Meng Chao about ten miles from Lo-yang, and in a heated battle, Lu Chi's forces were so severely decimated that it was said corpses dammed the Yangtze River. Lu was charged with treason, given a summary hearing, and executed. The summary executions of his two sons followed shortly thereafter. Lu Chi was forty-two.

He left some three hundred poems and several essays. Although well acquainted with the literati of his period, he was, apparently, a decidedly private man who numbered no close friends other than his younger brother, perhaps because of his barbed criticism. He once said of the highly touted Tso Ssu, "The old fool's writing a *fu* on each of the three capitals, but when he's done, they'll be good for nothing but wrapping a wine jug." Suspicious of fads and superficial literary reputations, he spent a lifetime studying the *Shih Ching (Poetry Classic)*, the *Analects, I Ching,* and Chuang Tzu and Lao Tzu. Echoes of such classics abound in the *Wen Fu*.

He lived in a society in which theology held virtually no sway. Although Buddhism had been imported from India in the first century, the Chinese mind held to practical social matters for the most part, joining aspects of Buddhist wisdom-teaching to practical Confucianism, just as it had made a marriage of Confucianism and Taoism. In China, it was often said, all things become Chinese. Only a hundred years later, under the inspired translations of Kumarajiva, would Buddhism, especially *Ch'an* or Zen, flower and flourish in China.

History as a formalized subject and program of study had been born with the composition of the *Tso chuan,* a long commentary mixing history and fiction and prophecy, in the fourth century B.C.E. The *Poetry Classic,* the *Chuang Tzu,* and others were studied from scrolls that were everywhere evident and much in demand. An "educated man" was expected to know the contents of "five cartloads." And because the first emperor of the Ch'in dynasty (200 B.C.E.) had attempted to purge all books but the *Book of Changes* or *I Ching,* the literate public was constantly protective of its libraries of irreplaceable scrolls. A scholar-poet's life could be dangerous almost by definition, and no doubt Master Lu felt a great sense of obligation to his tradition.

To this seriousness, Lu adds a *hsin,* or "heart/mind," which is unifying. Emotion and reason become one within the fully integrated personality. His culture recognized no distinction between poetry and reason. Nor did the classical Chinese literary mind distinguish between the rational and the irrational as clearly as we like to think we do.

The methodology of Confucius was rooted in what we in the West might call a Socratic tradition of dialogue between a "master" and several questioners. It is this style of inquiry Lu Chi brings to his rhymed poem on the art and use of letters. He answers questions before they can be asked. His lines are the lines of philosophy and aesthetics, irregular in length and rhythm, and rhymed—called rhymed prose or *fu*. While other poets of his time used the form in a kind of courtly bardic tradition, he turned it to decidedly other purposes, both in style of composition and intention.

Lu Chi's *fu* is that of the *p'ien wen* or "double harness" style; the poem depends upon a kind of parallelism, often moving two ways simultaneously through the deliberate use of ambiguity: "Things move into shadows and vanish; memory returns in an echo." The poet grounds his warnings and urgings in concrete imagery, often assuming that the reader's familiarity with Chinese music and/or literary classics runs as deeply as his own. In short, he wrote for a highly literate audience.

The word *wen* is among the oldest words in Chinese, going back at least three thousand years to the time of early shamanism and the oracle bones, where it meant, even then, *art,* including literary and plastic arts. In its most generic interpretation, *wen* means simply a pattern wherein meaning and form become inseparably united, so that they become one, indistinguishable. Furthermore, *wen* means "writing" or "literature" in the context of its being the most natural means of expression of the essential *hsin* (heart/mind) at the core of consciousness. *Wen* was most often written to mean "culture" in the broadest sense. Civilization is born with writing.

Just as Lu's discourse carries certain social connotations and implications, so his choice of the word *wen* carries a plurisignation; he calls forth the term to mean, specifically, literary arts. But literary arts cannot be entirely separated from social responsibilities to, for instance, tell the truth, which in Confucian society means to name things and events properly. He intends to write a defense of poesy that claims its use as utterly essential to civilization. Culture, in his mind and in his poem, "demands the use of letters."

Stephen Owen's elegant study, *Traditional*

Chinese Poetry and Poetics (University of Wisconsin Press, 1985), says this: "But in this formulation literature is not truly mimetic: rather it is the final stage in a process of manifestation; and the writer, instead of 're-presenting' the outer world, is in fact only the medium for this last phase of the world's coming-to-be."

A poet seeks personal and social transformation through poetry; the poet's art is both a gift *to* the writer and *from* the writer who understands that no great gift can be truly given or received in an emotional or intellectual void. All this is present in Lu Chi's poem on the coming-to-be-ness of a true writer.

By the time of the *Wen Fu,* China had already been two hundred years under the *san chiao* or "Three Doctrines" system. Buddhism, introduced in the first century, was, during Lu Chi's lifetime, the least influential. Taoism, like Confucianism, was primarily a philosophy, but had already been burdened with mystical rites and transcendental aspirations. Like Confucianism, it had become corrupted by the creation of vast bureaucracies and social conventions and the goofy rigors and demoralizing struggles of bogus gurus. Taoism also harbored its fortune-tellers and crypto-occultists, witches, and daemons.

Lu Chi appears to have concentrated his studies on the virtues of each of the three, preferring to ignore bureaucratic hierarchies, addressing the Taoist sense of *tzu-chan,* the idea of spontaneous origins, as the core inspiration of the process of writing. He would say that what we call the Void is only Mind. Daily discipline becomes—in practice—daily life. Study the past in order to become fully aware of the present, to fully inhabit the moment. Each day is new. In his insistence upon the right words in the right order, he followed the principles of Master K'ung. Spiritually, he reflects a tradition that would evolve into the *Ch'an* line of Buddhism. In attitude and in moral turpitude, he drew once again from the strengths of the *san-chiao* system, finding no apparent contradiction between his role as military leader and his inner, scholarly and spiritual life.

In the history of Chinese letters, Lu Chi holds a position similar to that of Aristotle in the West, but with one paramount distinction: virtually every

Chinese poet since the beginning of the fourth century has gone to school on the *Wen Fu,* and most memorized it. He is revered by traditionalist and experimentalist alike.

In the early 1950s, North American readers were treated to several reinventions of Lu Chi's famous treatise. E. R. Hughes published a large study that included a translation (Pantheon Books, 1951), but unfortunately failed—in the translation at least—to follow much of the advice of its author. Achilles Fang published a translation in the *New Mexico Quarterly* in the fall of 1952, and that same year, Shih-Hsiang Chen published yet another translation in an edition of four hundred copies at the Anthoesen Press in Portland, Maine, which was reprinted in Cyril Birch's *Anthology of Chinese Literature* (Grove Press, 1965).

These versions, along with Ezra Pound's famous comments on the Preface to the *Wen Fu,* have attracted and inspired many and various poets, including the title poem to Gary Snyder's *Axe Handles,* a poem "correcting" Ezra Pound's translation. But, as Lu Chi himself would be quick to point out, when cutting an axe handle with an axe, the model may indeed be at hand, as he says in the Preface, but the new axe handle, despite being modeled on the old, will be different. He directs us to look for the obvious model, knowing that no matter what we do with it, the fruits of our labors will differ from the original. Lu Chi's comments on axe handles are lifted directly from the *Shih Ching, Book I.*

Howard Nemerov's poem, "To Lu Chi," Eleanor Wilner's "Meditation on the *Wen-Fu*," and the title poem of Carolyn Kizer's 1965 collection, *Knock Upon Silence,* all result from those early translations.

Elegant simplicity and common sense, two of the rarest of attributes, distinguish Lu Chi's poem. It was never my intention to offer a strictly literal version of the *Wen Fu*. Much of the language of the original is simply mystifying to the average western reader coming to a text that is seventeen centuries old and rooted in the Chinese universe. My goal has been to use paraphrase or interpolation as judiciously as possible while remaining true to Lu Chi's ideals, to revision the poem in a western lyric mode, and to make it as I imagine he would if he were in the process of reinventing himself in another language and culture. This is of course a dangerous mode of procedure, but one followed by poets as early as those of the *Greek Anthology,* Catullus, and indeed Lu Chi himself in his own borrowings and interpretations from the *Shih Ching,* the *Lun Yu,* and dozens of other sources. The *Wen Fu* is the axe handle from which I model *The Art of Writing,* borrowing as he borrowed. The Japanese call this practice *honkadori,* borrowings from or deliberate echoes of classical poems. The Chinese no doubt have a similar term since they established the practice centuries earlier. Such are the roots of a noble tradition.

In practice, I've constructed a lyric paraphrase concentrating on what I perceive to be primary passages and images. In some places, I've condensed; in others, it has been necessary to make leaps or to slightly reorganize. If what I've made is of no practical use, I shall have brought Lu Chi and myself no honor. But if these teachings are indeed illuminating to one who struggles over a word or line, then due credit belongs not only with Master Lu, but with his commentators, both Oriental and Occidental, from whom I've learned.

A hundred years after Lu Chi composed his *Wen Fu,* the reclusive poet T'ao Ch'ien (also called T'ao

Yuan-ming), the acclaimed "grandfather of Chinese poetry," wrote a poem to his cousin, saying:

> Reading the classics again,
> sometimes I still find heroes,
>
> old sages I dare not emulate,
> but who stood strong in adversity.
>
> I too will not choose the easy way.

His poem echoes the advice of Lu Chi. He finds heroes he dares not emulate but who nonetheless set models and standards, both literary and ethical. Studying the "working of the minds" of these heroes, he clarifies his own thinking and thereby underscores his determination to follow within a defined tradition. In the preface to his poem "The Return," he says, "Whenever I have been involved in official life I was mortgaging myself to my mouth and belly, and the realization of this greatly upset me. I was deeply ashamed that I had so compromised my principles." (Translated by James Robert Hightower, *The Poetry of T'ao Ch'ien*, Oxford University Press, 1970.)

Just as Lu Chi chose to "bar the door" for a ten-year period of intense study, T'ao Ch'ien left

"official life" to return to his poor farm, his wife
and children often facing hunger, poverty, and political tribulations, but with his principles intact.
Both T'ao Ch'ien's bravery and his profound ethical accountability follow in the Confucian/Taoist
tradition Master Lu so luminously espoused. Lu
Chi and T'ao Ch'ien set standards that would be
followed by Tu Fu, Po Chu-i, and other major
Chinese poets, and by Japanese and Korean poets
as well, for centuries.

The *Wen Fu* remains as fresh and as demand-
ing for us all these centuries later as it was for the
great T'ao Ch'ien. One of Lu's masters from the
Confucian classics was old Master Tsung, who en-
graved on his bathtub, "Make it new, day by day,
make it new." In the late seventeenth century,
writing in the same tradition, Bashō advises his
students, "Nothing's worth seeing that is not seen
with fresh eyes."

Lu Chi was not interested in fostering a writing school or in establishing himself as the leader
of any particular literary movement. His aim was
to articulate the ethical and spiritual lineage of
great writers, to connect himself with predeces-
sors for whom the art of writing was neither easy

nor self-serving. He wanted to articulate the
whole inner life of the writer and the tradition.
And to understand what all that means within the
context of being fully alive to the here-and-now.

Sam Hamill
Kage-an
November 1999

THE ART OF

WRITING

PREFACE

When studying the work of the masters,
    I watch the working of their minds.

Surely, facility with language
    and the charging of the word with energy

are effects that can be achieved
    by various means.

Still, the beautiful can be distinguished
    from the common,
    the good from the mediocre.

Only through writing and then revising
    and revising
    may one gain the necessary insight.

We worry whether our ideas
    may fall short of their subjects,
    whether form and content rhyme.

This may be easy to know,
    but it is difficult
    to put into practice.

I have composed this rhymed prose
    on the art of writing
    to introduce

past masterpieces
    as models for an examination
    of the good and the bad in writing.

Perhaps it will one day be said
    that I have written
    something of substance,

something useful,
    that I have entered
    the mystery.

When cutting an axe handle with an axe,
    surely the model is at hand.

Each writer finds a new entrance
    into the mystery,
    and it is difficult to explain.

Nonetheless, I have set down my thinking as clearly as I can.

I. THE EARLY MOTION

The poet stands at the center
    of a universe,
    contemplating the enigma,

drawing sustenance
    from masterpieces of the past.

Studying the four seasons as they pass,
    we sigh;

seeing the inner-connectedness of things,
    we learn
    the innumerable ways of the world.

We mourn leaves torn away
    by the cruel hands of autumn;

we honor every tender
    bud of spring.

Autumn frost
    sends a shudder through the heart;
    summer clouds can make the spirit soar.

Learn to recite the classics;
    sing in the clear virtue
    of ancient masters.

Explore the treasures of the classics
    where form and content are born.

Thus moved, I lay aside my books
    and take writing brush in hand
    to compose this poem.

II. BEGINNING

Eyes closed, we listen
    to inner music,
       lost in thought and question:

our spirits ride
    to the eight corners of the universe,
       mind soaring a thousand miles away;

only then may the inner voice
    grow clear
       as objects become numinous.

We pour forth
    the essence of words,
       savoring their sweetness.

It is like being adrift
    in a heavenly lake
       or diving to the depths of seas.

We bring up living words
    like fishes hooked in their gills,
       leaping from the deep.

Luminous words are brought down
  like a bird on an arrow string
  shot from passing clouds.

We gather words and images
  from those unused
  by previous generations.

Our melodies
  have remained unplayed
  for a thousand years.

The morning blossoms bloom;
  soon, night buds will unfold.

Past and present commingle:
  Eternity
  in the single blink of an eye!

III. CHOOSING WORDS

Ordering thoughts and ideas,
    we begin to choose our words.

Each choice is made with care,
    fit with a sense of proportion.

Shadowy thoughts are brought
    into the light of reason;
    echoes are traced to their sources.

It is like following a branch
    to find the trembling leaf,
    like following a stream to find the spring.

The poet brings light into great darkness,
    even if that means the simple
    must become difficult or the difficult easy.

Hence, the tiger may silence other beasts,
    the dragon frighten away birds
    in terrifying waves.

Writing, the traveling
　　is sometimes level and easy,
　　sometimes rocky and steep.

Calm the heart's dark waters;
　　collect from deep thoughts
　　the proper names for things.

Heaven and earth are trapped in visible form:
　　all things emerge
　　from within the writing brush.

At first, the brush
　　parches our lips, but soon
　　it grows moist from dipping.

Truth is the tree trunk;
　　style makes beautiful foliage.

Emotion and reason are not two:
　　every shift in feeling must be read.

Finding true joy, find laughter;
in sorrow, identify each sigh.

Sometimes the words come freely;
sometimes we sit in silence,
gnawing on a brush.

IV. THE SATISFACTION

The pleasure a writer knows
    is the pleasure of sages.

Out of non-being, being is born;
    out of silence,
    a writer produces a song.

In one yard of silk, there is infinite space;
    language is a deluge
    from one small corner of the heart.

The net of images is cast wider
    and wider; thought searches
    more and more deeply.

The writer offers
    the fragrance of fresh flowers,
    an abundance of sprouting buds.

Bright winds lift each metaphor;
    clouds lift
    from a forest of writing brushes.

V. CATALOG OF GENRES

A body of writing may take any
    of a thousand forms,
      and there is no one right way to measure.

Changing, changing at the flick of a hand,
    its various forms are almost
    impossible to capture.

Words and phrases may compete
    with one another,
    but the mind is master.

Caught between the unborn and the living,
    a writer struggles to maintain
    both depth and surface.

One may depart from the square
    or overstep the circle searching for
    the one true form of one reality.

Great writing fills a reader's eyes
    with splendor
    and clarifies values.

One whose language remains muddled
    cannot do it; only when held in a clear mind
    can language become noble.

The lyric *[shih]* articulates
    speechless emotion, creating a fabric.

Rhymed prose *[fu]* presents
    its objects clearly.

Inscriptions *[pei]* must be simply written.

Elegies *[lei]* contain
    tangled webs of grief and so
    should be kept mournful.

Mnemonic poems *[ming]* must be simple,
    but also pregnant with meaning.

Admonitions *[chen]* cut against the grain
    and should therefore be written directly.

Eulogies *[sung]* are praises,
    but must demonstrate balance.

The treatise *[lun]* should be subtle,
   smooth, and polished.

Memorials *[tsou]* are simple and quiet,
   but carry highly polished elegance.

The discourse *[shuo]* should be both radiant
   and cunning.

Although each form is different,
   each opposes evil:
   none grants a writer license.

Language must speak from its essence
   to articulate reason:
   verbosity indicates lack of virtue.

VI. ON HARMONY

Each new composition assumes a special air,
    but only through trying many shapes and changes,
    learning the art of the subtle.

Ideas seek harmonious existence,
    one among others, through language
    that is both beautiful and true.

Sounds interlock and intermingle
    like the five colors of embroidery,
    each enhancing the others.

While it is true emotions are
    often capricious,
    indulgence is self-destructive.

Recognizing order
    is like opening
    a dam in a river.

Not-knowing is like grabbing
    the tail to direct the head
    of a dragon.

When dark and light are poorly mixed,
the result is always muddy.

VII. ON REVISION

Looking back, search for the disharmonious image;
    anticipating what may come,
    prepare a smooth transition.

Even with right reason, words
    sometimes clang; sometimes language flows,
    though the ideas themselves remain trivial.

Know one from the other
    and the writing will be clearer;
    confuse the two, and everything will suffer.

Art and virtue are measured
    in tiny grains.

The general inspects his men
    for every minutest detail,
    down to each single hair.

Only when revisions are precise
    may the building stand
    square and plumb.

VIII. THE KEY

While the language may be lovely
    and the reasoning just,

the ideas themselves
    may prove trivial.

What wants to continue must not end;
    what has been fully stated is
    itself a conclusion.

However each sentence
    branches and spreads,
    it grows from a well-placed phrase.

Restrain verbosity,
    establish order; otherwise,
    further and further revision.

IX. ON ORIGINALITY

The mind weaves elaborate
    tapestries with elegant,
    multicolored foliage.

The composition must move
    the heart like music
    from an instrument with many strings.

There are no new ideas,
    only those that rhyme
    with certain classics.

The shuttle has worked in my heart
    as it worked the hearts
    of those who came before me;

continuing the same
    warp and woof,
    I must make my fabric new.

Where truth and virtue are threatened,
    I must surrender
    even my favorite jewels.

X. SHADOW AND ECHO
AND JADE

Perhaps only a single blossom
    from the whole bouquet
    will bloom.

Perhaps only a single
    lonely cornstalk
    rises in the field.

Shadows cannot be held;
    echoes cannot be harnessed.

Poor work is an eyesore
    and obvious: it cannot
    be woven into music.

When the mind is caged and separate,
    the spirit wanders
    and nothing is controlled.

When the vein of jade
    is revealed in the rock,
    the whole mountain glistens.

Images must shine
    like pearls in water.

The thornbush, left unpruned,
    spreads in glorious disarray.

A common song
    sung to a great melody
    is another way to find beauty.

XI. FIVE CRITERIA

1. *Music*

When the rhythm is slack
    and has no tradition,
      the poem falters.

The poet searches in the silence
    for a friend,
      but finds none.

The poet calls and calls
    into the void,
      but nothing answers.

Heaven is out of reach —
    vast and empty.

A single weak note
    plucked on a lute
      cannot make beautiful music.

2. *Harmony*

When phrasing is lazy or self-indulgent,
   the music is gaudy,
      and no one will find beauty.

Where the beautiful mingles
   with the common,
      it is beauty that suffers.

One small blemish
   mars the whole beautiful face.

It is like hearing a harsh note from a flute
   from the courtyard below:
      it resonates out of tune.

One can make music
   and still lack all harmony.

3. *True Emotion*

Searching for a subject, a poet may indulge
    in the needlessly obscure or in the trivial,
    forsaking common sense.

Then all words will lack grace,
    they will ramble,
    and love will be betrayed.

As with the thinnest chords of the lute,
    one detects music and harmony
    that is present, yet resists definition.

Even though played in tune,
    the music may fail in its mission.

4. *Restraint*

Sometimes rhythms and harmonies
      dominate, and the poet
      finds them seductive.

Or, enchanted by the poet's
      voice, the crowd
      may shout hosannas.

Then vanity floods the eyes with the vulgar —
      a pretentious tune
      is unsuited to disciplined emotion.

It is like a bad musician who,
      to drown out imperfections,
      plays too loudly.

False feelings are
      a slap
      in the face of grace.

Even disciplined feeling
   leads nowhere
     unless there is also refinement.

5. *Refinement*

Only when the poem is free of false
    emotion and confusion
        will passions come into perspective.

Even then, the poem may be blander
    than sacrificial broth;
        it may be a blurred note from a broken string.

Hyperaware of technique,
    the poem may be stripped of its seasoning
    like a feast without gravy.

Or it may be good enough for
    "one to sing, three to praise"
    and still lack grace.

XII. FINDING FORM

Know when the work
    should be full,

and when it should be
    compacted.

Know when to lift your eyes
    and when to scrutinize.

Adapt to occasions as they arise;
    permit emotions to be subtle.

When the language is common,
    the image must be telling.

When the thinking is clumsy,
    the language must move smoothly.

Old clothes
    can be refurbished;

the stream we muddy
    soon runs itself clean again.

Only after looking and listening
    closely can one make

these various subtleties
    work their magic.

The sleeves of the dancers
    move with the melodies;

the singers' voices rise
    and fall with the music.

P'ien the Wheelwright
    tried to explain it,
    but he couldn't.

Nor can the artificial flowers of the critics
    explain it.

XIII. THE MASTERPIECE

I take the rules of grammar
    and guides to good language

and clutch them
    to heart-and-mind.

Know what is
    and what is not
    merely fashion;

learn what old masters
    praised highly,

although the wisdom of a subtle mind
    is often scoffed at
    by the public.

The brilliant semiprecious stones
    of popular fashion
    are as common as beans in the field.

Though the writers
    of my generation
    produce in profusion,

all their real jewels
    cannot fill the little cup
    I make of my fingers.

As infinite as space, good work
    joins earth to heaven;

it comes from nothing,
    like air through a bellows.

We carry the bucket from the well,
    but the bucket soon is empty.

Wanting every word to sing,
    every writer worries:

nothing is ever perfected;
    no poet can afford to become complacent.

We hear a jade bell's laughter
   and think it laughs at us.

For a poet, there is terror in the dust.

XIV. THE TERROR

I worry that my inkwell
    may run dry,

that right words
    cannot be found.

I want to respond to each
    moment's inspiration.

Work with what is given;
    that which passes
    cannot be detained.

Things move into shadows
    and vanish;
      memory returns in an echo.

When spring arrives,
    we know why nature has reasons.

Thoughts rise from the heart
    on breezes, and language
    finds its speaker.

Yesterday's buds
    are this morning's blossoms
    we draw with a brush on silk.

Every eye knows a pattern;
every ear hears distant music.

XV. THE INSPIRATION

The time comes when emotions
    strangle, though every stimulus
    demands response;

there are times
    when the spirit freezes.

The writer feels dead
    as bleached wood,
    dry as a riverbed in drought.

For a way out, search
    the depths of the soul
    for a spirit;

beg, if need be,
    for a vital sign of life.

The dark inside the mind
    lies hidden;

thoughts must be brought out
    like a child from the womb,
    terrified and screaming.

Forcing emotions
  brings error
  and error again;

letting them come
  naturally
  means letting them come clear.

The truth of the thing
  lies inside us,
  but no power on earth can force it.

Time after time,
  I search my heart in this struggle.

Sometimes a door slowly opens;
  sometimes the door
  remains bolted.

XVI. CONCLUSION

Consider the use of letters.
All principles demand them.

Though they travel a thousand miles or more,
nothing in this world can stop them.

They traverse the thousands of years.

Look at them one way,
and they clarify laws for the future.

Look at them another,
and they provide models from old masters.

The art of letters has saved governments
from ruin and propagates morals.

Through letters, there is no road
too difficult to travel,

no idea too confusing
to be ordered.

It comes like rain from clouds;
it renews the vital spirit.

Inscribed on bronze and marble,
it honors every virtue.

It sings in flute and strings
and every day is made newer.

A NOTE ON THE TRANSLATOR

Sam Hamill's celebrated translations include *Crossing the Yellow River: Three Hundred Poems from the Chinese; The Essential Chuang Tzu* (with J. P. Seaton); *Narrow Road to the Interior & Other Writings of Bashō; The Spring of My Life & Selected Haiku by Kobayashi Issa; River of Stars: Selected Poems of Yosano Akiko* (with Keiko Matsui Gibson); *Only Companion: Japanese Poems of Love & Longing; The Erotic Spirit;* and *The Infinite Moment: Poems from Ancient Greek.* He is the author of a dozen volumes of original poetry, including *Destination Zero: Poems 1970–1995* and *Gratitude,* as well as three collections of essays, including *A Poet's Work.* He is founding editor of Copper Canyon Press, director of the Port Townsend Writers' Conference, and contributing editor at *The American Poetry Review.*

THE COVER IMAGE

The ancient Chinese "patron saint" of letters, Kuei Hsing was renowned for great writing but cursed with a repugnant countenance. When it came time for the emperor to hand out literary certification at the capital, he found Kuei Hsing unbearable to look at. The poet was so humiliated that he threw himself into the river to drown. But he was carried into the heavens by a magical fish to live in a palace in the Big Dipper, where he became the arbiter of literature and calligraphy.

MORE POETRY
FROM MILKWEED EDITIONS

To order books or for more information,
contact Milkweed at (800) 520-6455
or visit our website (www.milkweed.org).

Turning Over the Earth
Ralph Black

Outsiders:
Poems about Rebels, Exiles, and Renegades
Edited by Laure-Anne Bosselaar

Urban Nature:
Poems about Wildlife in the City
Edited by Laure-Anne Bosselaar

Drive, They Said:
Poems about Americans and Their Cars
Edited by Kurt Brown

MILKWEED EDITIONS publishes with the intention of making a humane impact on society, in the belief that literature is a transformative art uniquely able to convey the essential experiences of the human heart and spirit. To that end, Milkweed publishes distinctive voices of literary merit in handsomely designed, visually dynamic books, exploring the ethical, cultural, and esthetic issues that free societies need continually to address. Milkweed Editions is a not-for-profit press.

Interior design by Elizabeth Cleveland
Typeset in Cochin 12/16
by Stanton Publication Services
Printed on 55# 100% postconsumer-waste paper
by Friesens Corporation